Death, Bu   S0-EIA-307
and Afterlife in
Ancient Egypt

Death, Burial, and Afterlife in Ancient Egypt

James F. Romano

The Brooklyn Museum

The Carnegie Museum of Natural History

This publication was made possible through a grant from the National Endowment for the Humanities, a federal agency.

Published by The Carnegie Museum of Natural History, Pittsburgh, PA 15213
Manufactured in the United States of America

ISBN 0-911239-19-7
Library of Congress Catalog Card Number: 89-85822

Front cover drawing: Anubis, patron god of embalmers, standing over the mummy of Sennedjem. Detail from a painting in Sennedjem's tomb. See figure 7.

Contents

About the Author

James F. Romano is Curator in the Department of
Egyptian, Classical, and Ancient Middle Eastern Art
at The Brooklyn Museum, where he has been em-
ployed since 1976. In addition to serving as an Adjunct
Lecturer in the Art History Department at Queens
College, he has been Chief Researcher in Egyptology
at the C. G. Jung Foundation and Research Intern at
the Metropolitan Museum of Art. In the winter of 1989
he received his Ph.D. in Ancient Near Eastern and
Egyptian Art and Archaeology from the Institute of
Fine Arts at New York University. He is the author
of numerous articles on ancient Egypt and coauthor of
several catalogues of Egyptian art.

Archaeologists have been excavating in Egypt for over a century. Their work has resulted in the discovery of thousands of burials, ranging in size from simple pits dug into the sand to vast multi-chambered subterranean structures several hundred feet long. Much of our knowledge of Egyptian funerary religion comes from analysis of offerings left in these burials as well as from the decoration and hieroglyphic texts inscribed or painted on the walls of large tombs.

Early Egyptologists were overly concerned with the material remains of Egypt's kings and ruling class. They devoted much of their attention to large tombs containing a wealth of valuable objects that would make attractive displays in the museums that sponsored their excavations. Only a few cemeteries belonging to groups we would call the Egyptian "middle class" have ever been excavated. Our knowledge of the society's lowest strata, including farmers, servants, and manual laborers, is even more meager. Not a single publication has ever described the systematic excavation of a lower-class cemetery of the historic period. Thus our picture of Egyptian funerary religion is heavily skewed to the tenets of the well-to-do. No doubt the beliefs of the common man echoed, to some degree, those of Egypt's upper class, but a detailed examination of lower-class perception of the afterlife must await future excavations.

Belief in the Afterlife

Archaeological evidence demonstrates that the ancient Egyptians had developed a belief in the

1. Naqada II burial of a man (ca. 3650–3300 B.C.). The grave goods include ceramic vessels, a slate palette, shell jewelry, an ivory comb, and a stone pot.

Carnegie Museum of Natural History diorama. Clockwise from bottom left: CMNH 9074-2303, 1168-44, 1168-34, 21537-20, 9074-2560, 1168-39, 21537-37, 9074-99999, 1168-16, 1168-23, 9074-2209a, 1948-55, 9074-2660i, 9074-2660e, 9074-2642; then center, 4210-4.

afterlife at least two thousand years before the first pyramid was built. Predynastic graves of the Badarian culture (ca. 4500–3800 B.C.) and the subsequent Naqada I and II cultures (ca. 3850–3300 B.C.) often contain simple offerings such as ceramic and stone vessels, jewelry, slate cosmetic palettes, and flint knives and tools (figure 1). Such household objects would have been included in a burial only if the population believed that they would be needed in a life after death. Since the Predynastic Egyptians lived before the invention of writing, they left no firsthand account of how they envisioned the hereafter. Because many Predynastic funerary offerings were used during life, Egyptologists presume that the earliest Egyptians saw the afterlife as very similar to their earthly existence.

With the founding of the Egyptian state at the beginning of Dynasty I (ca. 3100 B.C.), belief in the afterlife was reflected by the widespread appearance of monumental funerary architecture. Tombs of kings and nobles could be forty meters long and were filled with a vast array of gifts for the deceased deemed of potential use in a new existence. Texts from the Old Kingdom (Dynasty III–VI; ca. 2750–2250 B.C.) show that by the middle of the third millennium B.C., the Egyptians had formulated a series of funerary rituals and beliefs designed to guarantee that the spirit of the deceased would survive physical death.

Egyptian religion held that what we call the spirit or soul consisted of three distinct parts: the *ka*, *ba*, and *akh*. Egyptologists characterize the *ka* (represented by two upraised arms: ⊔) as the individual's "vital force" or "spiritual twin." When a person was born, the god Khnum created his or her *ka*, modeling both body and spirit on his potter's wheel. Kings could have several *ka*s; mere mortals had only one. During life the *ka* remained separate from the body. At death a person was said to have "gone to his [or her] *ka*." This was the Egyptian way of saying that the *ka* had merged with the deceased's lifeless form. To survive, the *ka* needed a body for its eternal home. The Egyptians believed that the *ka* dwelt within either the mummy or the tomb statue (sometimes called the *ka*-statue), a spare body needed if the corpse should be destroyed.

The *ka* also required sustenance in the form of food and drink. Without it the *ka* would cease to exist, ending any hope for life after death. Egyptians made elaborate provisions to see that their *ka*s would be tended after death. Funerary inscriptions frequently boast that the king or gods such as Osiris and Anubis would grant the tomb owner an eternal boon of "a thousand of bread, a thousand of beer, a thousand of cattle, and a thousand of fowl." Such gifts, whether real or symbolic, were rewards for loyalty and devotion. Representations and lists of food, wine, and beer on tomb walls were thought capable of sustaining the *ka*. Wealthier Egyptians entered into contractual arrangements with funerary priests (called *ka*-priests) who were paid by the tomb owner and his descendants to see that enough real provisions were periodically left in the tomb chapel. Respectful members of the deceased's family brought offerings to the tomb on a regular basis, particularly during major religious festivals.

Thus, by about 2675 B.C. the maintenance of the body and the perpetual offering of food and drink became the cornerstones of Egyptian funerary belief. Unless these duties were carried out, the soul could not achieve immortality.

The Egyptians called the second element of the soul the *ba* ("animation"; 𓅽). It was the part of the spirit

2. *Coffin fragment depicting a* ba-*bird.*

Gessoed wood. Height, 26 cm; width, 32 cm. Dynasty XXI, ca. 1070–945 B.C. Provenience unknown. CMNH, 2983-6551.

free to leave the tomb and travel about the earth during the day. The *ba* was obliged, however, to return to the tomb during the perilous hours of darkness. Artisans had several ways of showing the *ba*, but the most common took the form of a human-headed bird (figure 2). The *ba* came into being only when the *ka* and the dead body were united; without the *ka* and a mummy or *ka*-statue, the *ba* could not exist.

The third part of the Egyptian spirit, the *akh* (🐦; plural *akhu*), was never represented. The *akhu* lived in the sky, the realm of the gods. Specifically, the *akhu* were the circumpolar stars that never dipped below the horizon into the Egyptian underworld. Thus they were immortal. To become an *akh,* a spirit had to prove itself worthy before the gods. Once it did, it became an everlasting part of the universe.

Dwelling among the stars was only one of the many fates that could await an Egyptian spirit. The *ka* and *ba* were inexorably linked to the tomb's environs, experiencing a version of the afterlife resembling the deceased's earthly existence. Yet the soul could also be found in the underworld, the kingdom of Osiris (see below), or traversing the heavens in the barque of the sun god Re. Another popular belief maintained that spirits of the dead inhabited a place called *Amentet* ("the West"). The sun set every evening over the western horizon. To the Egyptians, this nightly disappearance signified the sun's death; the West thus became associated with dying. Perhaps the most ancient version of the soul's destiny held that after death the soul would inhabit an obscure place called the "Field of Reeds" or the "Field of Rushes."

The Egyptians' tendency to accept, seemingly without question, so many disparate notions of the afterlife reflects a key characteristic of their mentality. Ancient Egyptian culture existed for over three thousand years. During that time many religious concepts developed, including various apparently contradictory views of life after death. When a fresh, attractive idea came along, the Egyptians absorbed it into their body of traditional beliefs. However, they steadfastly adhered to their ancient teachings as well. In the context of Egyptian religion, one approach to immortality was not better than another. All beliefs were valid.

The Myth of Osiris

One funerary belief that underwent considerable change over the centuries was the myth of Osiris (figure 3). Since the complete story has not come down to us from a single source, Egyptologists must piece together the entire tale from numerous ancient writings. The so-called "Pyramid Texts," inscriptions carved on the walls of burial chambers in pyramids of Dynasty V and VI, provide the earliest telling of Osiris' travails.

Osiris was a wise and benevolent king of Egypt in Predynastic times. His brother Seth grew jealous of Osiris' power and popularity, tricked the king into entering a great ornate chest, sealed it, and threw it into the Nile drowning Osiris. But Isis, Osiris' wife, recovered her husband's lifeless form. When Seth learned of this, he seized the body, cutting it up into fourteen parts, which he scattered throughout Egypt. Isis and her sister, Nephthys, set out to collect the pieces of Osiris' corpse and found all but the penis. The two ladies fashioned a new phallus for the king. Using her magical powers, Isis restored Osiris to an animate existence, and they joined in sexual union, conceiving a son, the falcon-headed Horus.

Meanwhile Seth had usurped the Egyptian throne. Fearing his wrath, Isis and Horus hid in the marshes of the Nile Delta until the boy grew old enough to avenge his father's murder. So violent and disruptive was the ensuing battle between Horus and Seth that the gods of Egypt ordered a halt to the fighting, and the earth god Geb summoned a divine tribunal to hear the combatants' claims. Eventually the gods decided that Horus, the rightful heir of his father, would be

*3. Statuette of Osiris, ruler
of the underworld.*

*Bronze. Height, 22 cm;
width, 6.3 cm. Dynasty
XXVI, ca. 664-525 B.C.
Abydos. CMNH, 2231-19.*

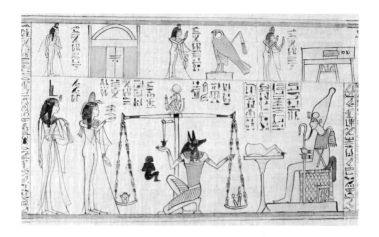

4. *Scene from the papyrus of the Lady Henet-tawy. Osiris, god of the dead, watches as the god Anubis adjusts the balance used to determine Henet-tawy's fate. Her heart rests on the left tray of the balance. On the opposite tray is the figure of Maat, the goddess of truth. If the balance remains even, Osiris will grant the lady eternal life.*

Painted papyrus. Height, 27.5 cm; width, 45 cm. Third Intermediate Period, Dynasty XXI, ca. 1070–945 B.C. From Deir el-Bahri. Metropolitan Museum of Art, 30.3.31, Rogers Fund, 1930.

king of Egypt, and Osiris, since he had died, must live forever in the underworld as god of the dead. There he presided at the judgment of the newly dead, deciding whether they were worthy of eternal life (figure 4).

In the Old Kingdom, this myth served as a model for royal succession. When a king died, he became the eternal Osiris and his replacement, the living Horus. Mortals in the Old Kingdom had no hope of becoming Osiris; they sought eternal life through other means. After the political and social chaos of the First Inter- mediate Period, the Middle Kingdom nobility began to usurp many royal prerogatives. One of these involved decorating their wooden coffins with versions of the Old Kingdom "Pyramid Texts," originally written to ensure that the king would become Osiris. These "Coffin Texts" gave certain members of Middle Kingdom society the potential for an Osirian afterlife.

Since the Egyptians believed that Osiris' head had been buried in Abydos, that Upper Egyptian town became the focal point of the god's cult. Beginning in the Middle Kingdom, pious pilgrims voyaged to Abydos and erected inscribed stone slabs, now called stelae. These monuments listed the dedicator's name, titles, and major accomplishments, calling them to Osiris' attention forever.

Even the humblest Egyptians were drawn to the image of the suffering Osiris, who, through the efforts of his wife and son, had gained immortality. They identified with the god so strongly that by the New Kingdom anyone could become Osiris if judged worthy. At this time a dead person was frequently referred to as "the Osiris so-and-so."

Development of Mummification

Since the quest for eternal life required the body's preservation, the Egyptians developed a system for maintaining the corpse. We call this procedure mummification, the form of embalming practiced by the ancient Egyptians. Actually, the term "mummy" is a misnomer. It derives from the tendency of Late Period embalmers to fill the body with molten resin. Corpses treated this way acquired a blackened appearance that

Egypt's Arab population thought resulted from immersion in bitumen. They called these shoddily embalmed bodies *mummiya*, the Arabic word for bitumen or pitch.

In its most developed form mummification involved four steps: (1) removing many of the internal organs, the first parts of the body to decompose, (2) drying the hollow body with natron, (3) filling the body cavity with stuffing and shaping it to restore the deceased's form and facial features, and (4) wrapping the body tightly in linen bandages.

Little is known of the beginnings of mummification. In the Predynastic Period bodies were placed in shallow, circular graves in the desert, away from precious arable land. They rested in a fetal position on their left side, their heads facing west. The early Egyptians made few provisions for separating the body from the sand. When sand came into contact with a newly buried body, natural mummification resulted. Body fluids, perhaps as much as 75 percent of a person's weight, were absorbed by the sand, leaving a gaunt, brownish, but lifelike corpse (see figure 1).

No doubt some of these burials were discovered by later generations of Predynastic Egyptians, perhaps when they inadvertently disturbed an old interment while burying their own dead. The natural appearance of their predecessors might have reassured them about their own fate and reinforced the desirability of preserving the body. Clearly, however, they drew no connection between the drying properties of sand and natural mummification. Toward the end of the Predynastic era, the Egyptians took steps to make the deceased's rest in the grave more comfortable. Graves were lined with mudbrick and plaster, and wooden beams served as roofing. Occasionally the body was

11

placed in a wooden coffin, perhaps an allusion to Osiris' chest. This elaboration in funerary ritual isolated the corpse from the desert sand. Ironically, bodies buried in these new, more commodious surroundings had no hope of an Egyptian afterlife. They quickly decomposed, and burials from this period are frequently little more than piles of bones.

In the first three dynasties (ca. 3100–2675 B.C.), Egyptians experimented with preservation, encasing bodies in tightly wrapped layers of resin-soaked bandages and shaping the linen over the face and body to resemble the deceased. Since these ancients took no steps to retard the decomposition of the flesh and internal organs, this technique proved unsuccessful. Bodies of Dynasty I–III prepared in this way often survive only as hardened linen shells containing loose bones.

True mummification began in the early part of Dynasty IV (ca. 2675–2565 B.C.), when the people charged with preparing the dead for burial came to realize the necessity of removing the vital organs. The stomach, liver, lungs, and intestines were the first parts of the body to decompose. By extracting them, the embalmers retarded the body's natural decomposition. At precisely this time the Egyptians abandoned the traditional fetal position in favor of fully extended burials. Presumably this change was made to facilitate the removal of the viscera through the abdomen.

Old Kingdom embalmers paid considerable attention to making the mummy as lifelike as possible. Stuffing such as straw, sawdust, and linen was placed inside the body and fashioned into a realistic shape. Funerary workers used black paint to highlight facial details including the eyebrows and mustache.

For nearly two thousand years embalmers modified the techniques of their art. In the Middle Kingdom

tiny pieces. These were then scooped out through the nose using a device resembling a tiny ladle, and the empty skull was filled with stuffing. The Egyptians saw no reason to preserve the brain and simply discarded all the bits they extracted.

Next, the embalmers removed four of the vital organs—the stomach, intestines, liver, and lungs—usually through a small incision on the left side of the abdomen. First the stomach, liver, and intestines were pulled through. Then the embalmers punctured the diaphram, allowing access to the lungs. After removing these organs, they rinsed the hollow chest and abdomen, using, according to Herodotus, palm wine.

Since the deceased would need these organs in the afterlife, they were not discarded. Sometimes the viscera were neatly wrapped in resinous packages and put inside the mummy. The more common technique required the embalmers to place the four organs in so-called canopic jars that were stored in a chest within the tomb. Old Kingdom canopic jars frequently have plain lids; Middle Kingdom examples come with stoppers in the form of human heads. During early Dynasty XVIII artisans began manufacturing jars with lids bearing images of the four "Sons of Horus," the divine guardians of the viscera. The human-headed god Imset protected the liver; Duamutef, shown with a dog or jackal head, safeguarded the deceased's stomach; Hapy, responsible for the lungs, had the form of an ape; and Qebehsenef, who guarded the intestines, appears as a falcon (figure 8).

The embalmers did not remove all vital organs. Since the Egyptians considered the heart the seat of human intelligence, they took great pains to see that it was left in the body. In the New Kingdom religious texts called the "Book of the Dead" recounted three spells

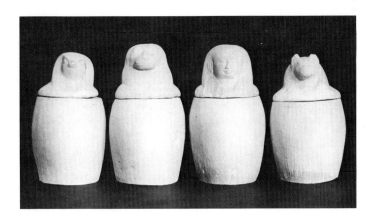

8. Canopic jar set, depicting the four sons of Horus. Left to right: Qebehsenef, Hapy, Imset, and Duamutef.

Limestone. Height, 26.5 to 29 cm; diameter, 15.1 to 15.7 cm. Late Period, Dynasty XXVI, ca. 664–525 B.C. Provenience unknown. CMNH, 15673-5, 3, 2, and 4.

intended to guarantee that the embalmers would not accidentally remove the heart.

At this point the body was ready for the all-important drying process. Workers filled it with temporary stuffing to preserve its original contours. For expensive burials they used bags of natron; they placed straw, wood shavings, or reeds in the mummies of poorer individuals. The corpse then rested on a slightly sloping embalming table, where it remained for forty days under a pile of liquid-absorbing natron.

At the end of this period, workers removed the fully dehydrated body from the table and extracted, but did not discard, the temporary stuffing. The interior was once again cleansed and allowed to dry. Then began the body's final packing. The ultimate appearance of the mummy depended on the skill of the embalmers responsible for this stage. If too much stuffing was used, the pressure it exerted on the flesh might cause

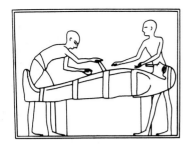

9. Embalmers applying resin to a mummy.

Drawing of painting from tomb of Amenemipet at Thebes (Tomb No. 41). New Kingdom, Dynasty XIX, reign of Ramesses II, ca. 1279–1213 B.C.

unsightly cracking, endangering the wholeness of the body and, thus, the hope for immortality. The skin's original suppleness was partially restored by covering the body with a mixture of milk, wine, spices, beeswax, natron, and juniper oil. The embalmers inserted linen or wax plugs into the nostrils, ears, and mouth; the eyes were pushed down into their sockets, with linen or lifelike stone eyes placed in the cavities. Workmen brushed on a final layer of resin making the body impervious to moisture (figure 9).

Just before wrapping the body, the embalmers turned it over to cosmeticians who applied layers of rouge to the cheeks, covered the head with a braided wig, and sometimes even dressed the deceased in his or her finest jewelry and clothing. The mummy was now ready for wrapping.

This process normally required fifteen days, much of which was spent in prayer. Since the Egyptians viewed the final bandaging of the mummy as fraught with danger, they created a very deliberate ritual requiring that nearly every twist of the wrappers' arms be accompanied by a solemn prayer or magical incantation. At this time priests placed charms called amulets on the mummy between the layers of linen bandages. The most important was laid over the heart; this amulet had

a

b

---

10. Two heart scarabs (a and b) and an amulet (c) in the form of a human heart. The inscriptions on the bottom of these pieces contain the text of Chapter XXXb of the "Book of the Dead." This spell was intended to guarantee that the embalmers would not accidentally remove the deceased's heart during mummification.

(a) Steatite with inscription on gold foil. Dynasty XXVI, ca. 664–525 B.C. Said to be from Saqqara. The Brooklyn Museum, 37.717E, Charles Edwin Wilbour Fund.
(b) Jasper (?). New Kingdom, ca. 1539–1070 B.C.

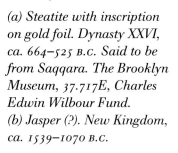

c

Provenience unknown. The Brooklyn Museum, 37.481E, Charles Edwin Wilbour Fund. (c) Dark green stone. New Kingdom or later, ca. 1539–664 B.C. Provenience unknown. The Brooklyn Museum, 37.479E, Charles Edwin Wilbour Fund.

11. A group of amulets.

Left to right, top to bottom:
Wedjet-*eye; faience;*
Dynasty XXVI–XXXI, ca.
664–332 B.C.; Sharona;
CMNH, 2400-29. Scarab;
faience; early Dynasty XVIII,
ca. 1479–25 B.C.; Abydos,
D116; CMNH 1917-60.
Heart; glass; New

Kingdom–Late Period, ca.
1539–332B.C.; provenience
unknown; CMNH 33898-2.
The god Shu; faience;
Dynasty XXVI–XXXI, ca.
664–332 B.C.; provenience
unknown; CMNH 1867-8a.
The god Re-Horakhty;
faience; early Dynasty XVIII,
ca. 1479–25 B.C.; Abydos,
D116; CMNH 1917-61.

the form of a scarab beetle or human heart. Such heart scarabs and heart-shaped amulets (figure 10) were normally carved in green stone and inscribed with spells for preventing the deceased's heart "from creating opposition against him." Other amulets, commonly found on top of the mummy or wrapped within its bandages, included the *wedjet*-eye (the "Eye of Horus"), tiny hearts, *djed*-pillars of Osiris, and figures of the "Sons of Horus" (figure 11).

Once all the sacred utterances were spoken and the mummy's bandages wound so that the form of the body was preserved, the embalmers' task was completed. Seventy days after the deceased "went to his *ka*," the guardians of the secrets of Anubis returned the mummy to the family for burial.

Tombs and the Burial

At this point the mummy was ready to be placed in its tomb. All ancient Egyptian tomb architecture shared a common feature: The body was placed in a subterranean burial chamber. Superstructures, however, showed a wide variety of forms. Burials of the Predynastic Period, for example, probably featured low mounds of stone that served the dual function of protecting the corpse from scavengers and marking the spot so family members could leave food. All later tomb architecture sought to solve the twin problems of safeguarding the body and providing a way for the spirit to receive and partake of offerings.

In Dynasty I low mudbrick retaining walls were laid out in a rectangle surrounding the opening of a deep shaft leading to the burial chamber. Workers filled the space within these walls with rubble or bricks, blocking access to the mummy. The resulting rectangular mounds, which resembled benches seen in front of modern Egyptian houses, are called mastabas after the Arabic word for bench (figure 12). Mastaba tombs enjoyed great popularity in the Old and Middle Kingdoms, particularly in the northern part of Egypt. Many mastabas had two shafts and burial chambers, for hus-

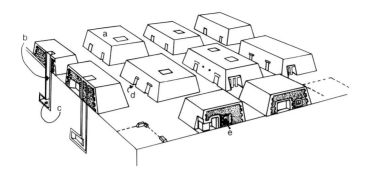

12. Artist's reconstruction of an Old Kingdom mastaba field. Egyptian architects often layed out mastaba cemeteries in a grid pattern with narrow "streets" between tombs. Each mastaba had a superstructure (a) that was pierced by a burial shaft (b) leading to the burial chamber (c). A doorway (d) on the mastaba's east side provided access to the chapel; within the chapel was the serdab (e) for the ka-statue.

band and wife. Early examples often featured a pair of niches on the eastern exterior wall. Over time architects increased the depth of the southern recess until it extended well into the mastaba's superstructure as a small chapel. There the family and ka-priests could present food offerings to the deceased.

Throughout the Old Kingdom architects designed larger and larger chapels until the original single room became a series of chambers honeycombing the superstructure. The layout of these tombs resembled great houses (figure 13). Artisans decorated the interior walls with relief carvings showing food offerings and images of the deceased seated before a table heaped with bread, meat, and vegetables. Representations of daily activities were also found in abundance. Such scenes provided the spirit with a familiar environment it could enjoy throughout eternity.

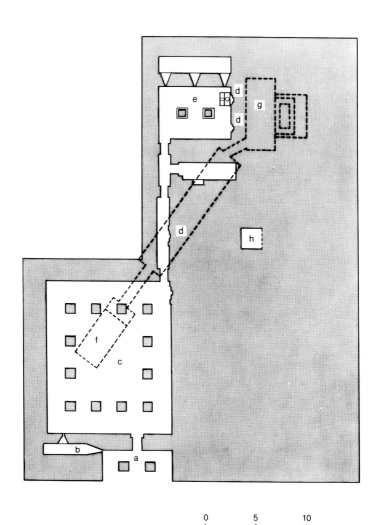

0   5   10

13. Plan of the mastaba of the official Ti and his wife Nefer-hetep-es at Saqqara (late Dynasty V, ca. 2390–2345 B.C.). The principal features of this mastaba include: (a) entrance to chapel, (b) serdab, (c) pillared hall, (d) false door, (e) chapel, *(f) shaft leading to Ti's burial chamber, (g) Ti's burial chamber, and (h) Nefer-hetep-es' burial chamber. Not all Old Kingdom mastabas had such complex plans. The pillared hall, for example, appears in only the most elaborate tombs.*

Within this complex of rooms artisans carved a representation of a door (figure 14). This "false door," which normally appeared on the wall immediately backing the burial shaft, provided the *ka* with access into the chapel where it would find nourishment. The *ka*-statue, the *ka*'s spare body, was enclosed within a chamber called a *serdab*. Architects, always mindful of the *ka*'s need to move freely, frequently left a small slit in the wall separating the *serdab* from the chapel.

In areas with steep cliffs, the Egyptians tended to cut tombs deep into the native rock. These rock-cut tombs varied greatly in size. Most had a long chapel, often with at least one *ka*-statue in a central niche directly opposite the door. A deep shaft descended from the chapel to the burial chamber. Elaborate rock-cut tombs featured additional rooms decorated with religious imagery and scenes of daily life (figure 15).

These rock-cut tombs first appeared in the Old Kingdom and came to typify New Kingdom tomb design. The cemetery at Deir el-Medina contains some of the finest rock-cut tombs, featuring deep subterranean passageways leading to vaulted, richly painted burial chambers (figure 16). Representations of the facades show small chapels capped with pyramids (figure 17).

As a general rule Egyptians lived on the Nile's east side and buried their dead in the low desert of the west bank. On the morning of the funeral the deceased's survivors would leave their homes for a boat voyage to the West, the land of the dead. Professional mourners accompanied the group, pulling their hair, throwing dust into the air and on their faces, and falling to the ground in carefully orchestrated demonstrations of grief (figure 18).

Servants carried lavish floral bouquets, food offerings, jars of water and wine, and containers of sacred

14. False door in Mereruka's tomb at Saqqara.

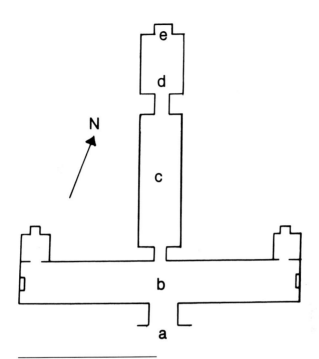

*15. Plan of the rock-cut
tomb of Amunedjeh in
western Thebes (Dynasty
XVIII, ca. 1479–1425 B.C.).
The entrance (a) leads into a
broad hall (b) and a long
passageway (c). At the end of
the passage is the chapel (d)
with the statue niche (e) in
the wall directly opposite the
tomb entrance.*

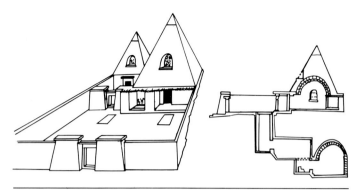

16. *Reconstruction and section of a private tomb at Deir el-Medina (late New Kingdom, Dynasty XIX–XX,* ca. 1295–1070 B.C.). *The tomb is capped by a brick pyramid; the burial chamber is vaulted.*

17. *Detail of coffin fragment with decoration depicting a man making offerings to a mummy in front of its pyramid-capped tomb.*

Painted wood. Fragment height, 22 cm; width, 48 cm.

Detail height, 13.5 cm; width, 18.5 cm. Third Intermediate Period, Dynasty XXI, ca. 1070–945 B.C. Provenience unknown. CMNH, 9074-2429.

18. Tomb scenes frequently
show professional mourners
participating in the
deceased's funeral.

Relief. Limestone. Height,
27.2 cm; width, 38.5 cm.

Dynasty XIX, ca. 1295–1185
B.C. From Saqqara. The
Brooklyn Museum, 37.31E,
Charles Edwin Wilbour
Fund.

oils (figure 19). Ritual objects intended for burial were
brought as well. The most important included the
canopic jars, usually placed in a large box, and a
chest containing funerary figures called *shabtis* (also
called *shawabtis* or *ushebtis*) (figure 20). These statu-
ettes would guarantee the deceased a leisurely afterlife.
Should the soul be called upon to plow fields, scatter
seed, or transport sand, it would turn to a *shabti* (from
the ancient word meaning "those who answer") who
would act as a substitute laborer. To guarantee that
their *shabtis* would work, the ever-practical Egyptians
often made "overseer *shabtis*," recognizable by their
skirt and whip.

From the New Kingdom on, more elaborate burials

19. *The bald offering bearer carries a box laden with onions and other vegetables. His companion has a tray with three vessels containing liquid offerings for the deceased.*

Relief. Limestone. Height, 31.7 cm; width, 92.7 cm. Early Dynasty XIX, ca. 1295–1250 B.C. Provenience unknown, probably from Saqqara. The Carnegie Museum of Art, 72.18.1.

included a "Book of the Dead" papyrus, a collection of nearly 200 spells to overcome any dangers that might arise in the afterlife, hymns to various gods, and incantations to make the mummy's amulets effective. "Book of the Dead" papyri were often placed in a wooden box surmounted by a figure of the composite god Ptah-Sokar-Osiris (figure 21).

When the cortège reached the Nile it crossed the river in an elaborate funerary barque. Its destination was the place of embalming, located on the west bank probably quite near the cemetery, where the body had been prepared for burial. After collecting the mummy, members of the funeral placed it on a sled and dragged it to its final home, the tomb or "house of the *ka*."

At the tomb entrance a priest, called the *sem*, began the Opening of the Mouth ceremony, an ancient rite that magically restored the mummy's senses. The *sem*-priest touched the mummy with several amuletic objects and placed the right foreleg of a freshly slaugh-

20. *Six* shabtis *from various periods of ancient Egypt.*

Left to right: Wood; late New Kingdom, ca. 1295–1070 B.C.; provenience unknown; CMNH, 2983-6771. Painted ceramic; late New Kingdom, ca. 1295–1070 B.C.; Abydos; CMNH, 1662-10. Painted limestone; mid Dynasty XVIII, ca. 1479–1400 B.C.; Abydos; CMNH, 1917-445.

Faience; Dynasty XXVI, ca. 664-525 B.C.; provenience unknown; CMNH 11983-8. Painted ceramic; Third Intermediate Period, ca. 1070–653 B.C.; provenience unknown; CMNH, 2983-6747. Faience; Third Intermediate Period, ca. 1070–653 B.C.; provenience unknown; CMNH 9007-37. Heights range from 6.4 cm to 17.8 cm.

tered ox to the mummy's mouth. The ritual was re-peated before the *ka*-statue, enabling it to function in place of the mummy should the need arise.

Now the mummy was ready to be placed in a coffin. The appearance of coffins and even the material used to make them changed over the three thousand years of Egyptian civilization. Rectangular wooden varieties enjoyed great popularity in the Old and Middle King-doms. In the latter period, artisans painted *wedjet*-eyes

21. Statuette of the funerary god Ptah-Sokar-Osiris.

Gessoed wood. Height, 54.8 cm; width, 17 cm; depth, 30.4 cm. Late Period,

Dynasty XXVI–XXXI, ca. 664–332 B.C. Provenience unknown. CMNH, 9074-2462a.

on the left side and frequently added short prayers invoking numerous gods including Osiris, Geb (the earth god), and Nut (Mistress of the Sky). If the deceased was wealthy, the wooden coffin might have been placed within a granite or calcite container called a sarcophagus (figure 22).

The Egyptians began making coffins in anthropomorphic form during the Middle Kingdom, and by the New Kingdom human-shaped coffins had completely superseded the rectangular variety. Their surfaces were covered with hieroglyphic texts and painted images borrowed from the "Book of the Dead." Coffins could be made of wood or an inexpensive mixture of linen and plaster called cartonnage, which the Egyptians could easily model into the shape of a body. Sarcophagi began appearing in human form during this time as well. At the beginning of the Third Intermediate Period, in Dynasty XXI, anthropoid coffins had few inscriptions other than the deceased's name and titles. Instead, the exterior was covered with a profusion of religious symbols (figure 23). By the Late Period and Ptolemaic era stone carvers produced huge limestone and granite sarcophagi, many in human form (figure 24).

Once the coffin or sarcophagus was closed and lowered into the burial chamber, servants stacked the tomb's interior with the funerary offerings and ritual equipment. Priests offered final prayers, the shaft leading to the burial chamber was filled with rubble, and the tomb was shut and sealed. Outside the tomb, the members of the funerary procession turned their attention to a banquet arranged for them while they attended the mummy. The meal consisted of meat, fowl, and wine; and in the more elaborate repasts participants adorned themselves with floral collars. After the

22. *This granite sarcophagus belonged to Prince Akhethotep, the son of Pharaoh Khufu (Dynasty IV). The exterior features a decoration of recessed panels echoing the facade of the Royal Palace. This imagery was appropriate since the sarcophagus was to be the prince's "home" for eternity.*

Red granite. Length, 2.37 cm; height, 1.30 m; width, 1.05 cm. Old Kingdom, Dynasty IV, reign of Pharaoh Khafre, ca. 2540–2500 B.C. From Giza. The Brooklyn Museum, 48.110, Charles Edwin Wilbour Fund.

23. *Coffin belonging to a "Chantress of Amun." This title, common for women in Dynasty XXI, implies an association with the local temple dedicated to the god Amun.*

Gessoed wood. Length, 1.94 m; width, 54 cm. Third Intermediate Period, Dynasty XXI, ca. 1070–945 B.C. Provenience unknown. CMNH, 1b and c.

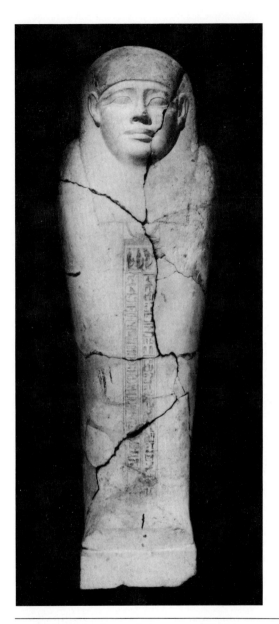

24. *This sarcophagus lid belonged to Mehetdiesnakht who was a sistrum player for the cult of Bastet. Limestone. Length, 200 cm;* *width, 66 cm; thickness, 36.5 cm. Dynasty XXX–early Ptolemaic Period, ca. 380–200 B.C. Abydos. CMNH, 1917-472.*

banquet, the dishes and cups were deliberately broken and the pieces, as well as any food remains, buried near the tomb entrance.

Only one other task remained. All the instruments and temporary packing used by the embalmers in preparing the mummy had to be buried close to the tomb. Egyptian belief required that the body be, quite literally, whole. If so much as a scrap of flesh or a single hair had adhered to any of the embalming equipment and the spirit was unable to retrieve it, the deceased's hope for eternal life after death would have been diminished.

Conclusion

As the family members left the necropolis, no doubt their thoughts centered on the loved one who now dwelt in the hereafter. The most reflective of them may have also contemplated their own views of life after death.

Throughout their lifetime, the Egyptians prepared for death. They built tombs and assembled funerary offerings that would serve them in the next life. But it would be an unfortunate oversimplification to say that the Egyptians were obsessed with death. They *were* obsessed with completeness. The Egyptians believed that any task, whether furnishing a tomb, decorating the walls of a temple, or building a pyramid, had to be meticulously planned and thoroughly executed. The great care they lavished on the corpse and its surroundings simply reflects the Egyptians' belief that if something was not complete, it was not good.

The dead were thought capable of mischief, and

mysterious illnesses were occasionally seen as the malignant influence of an unfriendly spirit. However, there is no evidence to suggest that the ancient Egyptians universally feared or avoided the dead. They composed letters to deceased family members, occasionally asking their departed ancestors to intercede on their behalf to solve mundane problems. Certainly the great number of tomb robberies carried out in ancient Egypt shows that some elements of society, at least, saw the souls of the dead as incapable of retribution.

Inscriptions from the Pharaonic Period do indicate, however, that the Egyptians had a strong fear of death and dying. A text frequently found in the entrances of Egyptian tombs succinctly expresses the ancients' contrasting feelings toward life and death. It calls on passersby to remember the tomb owner and beckons them as "ye who love life and hate death."

Certainly some of this aversion can be explained as fear of the unknown. In general, the Egyptians saw death as an interruption of life and the afterlife as an accurate replica of their earthly condition and, as such, something they could fathom with relative ease. But there were elements to life-after-death that the Egyptians could neither understand nor consider without great trepidation. They saw their hereafter as filled with dangers that could deprive the *ka* of eternal life. If the mummy or tomb statue were damaged or destroyed, if the deceased's name were somehow forgotten, if the appropriate offerings were not left, or if the *ka*-priests neglected their responsibilities to the funerary cult, the *ka* would cease to function as an animate force with ties to the living. Rather, it would face an eternity of dark, formless oblivion. This was the ancient Egyptians' ultimate fear.

Suggested Reading

Andrews, Carol. *Egyptian Mummies*. Cambridge,
   Massachusetts: Harvard University Press, 1984.
Dawson, W.R., and P.H.K. Gray. *Catalogue of
   Egyptian Antiquities in the British Museum*. Vol. I,
   Mummies and Human Remains. London: British
   Museum Publications, 1968.
Faulkner, R.O. *The Egyptian Coffin Texts*. 3 vols.
   Warminster, England: Aris & Phillips, 1973–1977.
Faulkner, R.O. *The Ancient Egyptian Book of the
   Dead*. London: British Museum Publications, 1985.
Fleming, Stuart; Bernard Fishman; David O'Connor;
   and David Silverman. *The Egyptian Mummy:
   Secrets and Science*. Philadelphia: University
   Museum, 1980.
Gardiner, Alan H. *The Attitude of the Ancient
   Egyptians to Death and the Dead*. Cambridge,
   England: Cambridge University Press, 1935.
Hamilton-Paterson, James, and Carol Andrews.
   Mummies: Death and Life in Ancient Egypt.
   Harmondsworth, England: Penguin Books, 1978.
Harris, James E., and Kent R. Weeks. *X-Raying the
   Pharaohs*. London: Macdonald, 1973.
Harris, James E., and Edward F. Wente. *An X-Ray
   Atlas of the Royal Mummies*. Chicago: University of
   Chicago Press, 1980.
Hayes, William C. *Scepter of Egypt*. 2 vols.
   Cambridge, Massachusetts: Harvard University
   Press, 1953, 1959.

James, T.G.H. *An Introduction to Ancient Egypt.* New York: Farrar Straus Giroux, 1979.

Lloyd, Alan B. *Herodotus, Book II, Commentary 1–98.* Leiden, Netherlands: Brill, 1976.

Schneider, Hans. *Shabtis.* 3 vols. Leiden, Netherlands: Rijksmuseum van Oudheden, 1977.

Spencer, A.J. *Death in Ancient Egypt.* Harmondsworth, England: Penguin Books, 1982.

Acknowledgments

Front cover. Drawing by Linda A. Witt.

Figs. 1–3, 6, 8, 11, 17, 20, 21, 23, and 24. CMNH photographs by M. McNaugher.

Figs. 4 and 5. Courtesy of the Metropolitan Museum of Art, all rights reserved.

Figs. 7 and 14. CMNH photos.

Fig. 9. Line drawing adapted by N. Perkins from *The Journal of Egyptian Archaeology* 16:1927, plate XVIII.

Figs. 10, 18, and 22. Courtesy of The Brooklyn Museum.

Figs. 12 and 16. Line drawings adapted by N. Perkins from E.B. Smith, *Egyptian Architecture as Cultural Expression* (New York: D. Appleton-Century, 1938), plate XXI.

Fig. 13. Line drawing adapted by N. Perkins from G. Steindorff, *Das Grab des Ti* (Leipzig: J.C. Hinrichs'sche Buchhandlung, 1913), plate I.

Fig. 15. Line drawing adapted by N. Perkins from B. Porter and R.L.B. Moss, *Topographical Bibliography of Ancient Egyptian Hieroglyphic Texts, Reliefs, and Paintings*, I, *The Theban Necropolis, Part 1, Private Tombs*, 2nd ed. (Oxford, England: Griffith Institute, Ashmolean Museum, 1970), page 160.

Fig. 19. Courtesy of The Carnegie Museum of Art.